HOW TO RAISE AND TRAIN A SPITZ

By Ernest H. Hart

SO-AIH-846

Distributed in the U.S.A. by T.F.H. Publications, Inc., 211 West Sylvania Avenue, P.O. Box 27, Neptune City, N.J. 07753; in England by T.F.H. (Gt. Britain) Ltd., 13 Nutley Lane, Reigate, Surrey; in Canada to the book store and library trade by Clarke, Irwin & Company, Clarwin House, 791 St. Clair Avenue West, Toronto 10, Ontario; in Canada to the pet trade by Rolf C. Hagen Ltd., 3225 Sartelon Street, Montreal 382, Quebec; in Southeast Asia by Y.W. Ong, 9 Lorong 36 Geylang, Singapore 14; in Australia and the south Pacific by Pet Imports Pty. Ltd., P.O. Box 149, Brookvale 2100, N.S.W., Australia. Published by T.F.H. Publications Inc. Ltd., The British Crown Colony of Hong Kong.

Cover painting by the Author

Frontispiece: The Spitz has survived as a distinct breed for many decades without the official sanction of many breed registries. The fact that he has done so well without this is a testimonial to the high esteem in which he is held by his legion of friends.

Photography by Louise Van der Meid

ISBN 0-87666-397-8

Contents

1. History and Description

The Spitz dog has had many names in America; "Wolf" Spitz, "Eskimo" Spitz, "Chow" Spitz, and "German" Spitz, among others. But they have all been applied to the same breed, a breed that mirrors a very old canine type, the Spitz. Mid-Victorian fanciers realized the basic value of the Spitz and took the breed to its heart. The breed later lost some of its pristine popularity as many other breeds of dogs came into vogue, were pushed by their fancy into recognition by the American Kennel Club, and were then exhibited at shows where the public could become aware of their many qualities.

But, for some obscure reason, no powerful groups or enterprising clubs formed to forward the cause of the Spitz. To the author this is indeed an enigma, for the Spitz certainly has as many fine qualities as most of the other recognized breeds of dogs. As a matter of fact, most owners and breeders of Spitz dogs will tell you vehemently that there is no finer breed of canine in all dogdom than the Spitz. Perhaps it was and is because the

Wee Minute Man, owned by Mell-O-Bark Kennels, typifies everything that is desirable in a typical Spitz. Sparkling, dark eyes that stand in striking contrast to the full, white coat are essentials that enhance the beauty of these lovely dogs.

Little Sheba, owned by Mr. and Mrs. Thomas N. McCoy, serves her family well by reason of her wonderful companionship and keen, alert nature. It is this natural keenness that has given the breed a reputation as a watchdog second to none.

Spitz is owned by the type of people who don't care about exhibiting their animals, and just want to contentedly live with them and keep them as pets and house dogs, at which jobs the breed certainly shines.

As a result of this phlegmatic attitude toward official recognition by the Spitz fancy, the breed cannot be registered with the American Kennel Club since it has not been recognized as a pure breed worthy of taking its place in the accepted family of purebred dogs. It follows that neither can it be shown in dog shows sponsored by the American Kennel Club to spark breed competition and truer breeding toward an ideal.

There are, of course, other registering bodies, and the Spitz dog has been accepted as a purebred dog by one of these, the United Kennel Club.

GENEALOGY OF THE SPITZ

In a time long before history, there was a mammal called *Tomarctus*, a long bodied, short-legged predator that was the first true dog, the father of the dog family. From Tomarctus there came four types of canines that we call the basic prototype canines, for from this quartet originated the family basis for all the many and varied breeds of dogs we know today.

One of these four prototype dogs, *Canis familiaris intermedius*, is important to us because from it came the early northern dogs, the sled dogs, and of this imposing group of canines the Spitz is one of the most important. As a matter of fact the Spitz can itself be termed a "prototype" dog, because from it there evolved many other breeds, well-known and varied breeds such as: the Pomeranian, the Samoyed, the Schipperke, the Keeshond, Norwegian Elkhound, Chow Chow, and the many Northern sled dogs, including the Eskimo, Siberian Husky, and Malamute, among others.

In other countries such as Germany and Finland, the Spitz is a recognized breed and is larger than the modern American Spitz. One type, the Finnish Spitz, is of a reddish color and is a recognized breed in Great Britain. As a matter of fact the Spitz in America was a larger dog earlier in its history, and in the early part of the twentieth century (1920, etc.) the American Spitz weighed from 25 to 30 pounds. Before the turn of the century the Spitz was truly a popular dog in this country.

But long before the breed came to this continent, long before history and the knowledge that continents existed, man and dog found each other, helped each other, and shaped the friendship and companionship that would endure for thousands of years.

As mankind developed in the long process of evolution, and the scales of survival tipped from beast to human, so the dog developed, too. At first the dog was a hunter, as was man. Then, when man became a shepherd, so did the dog. The earth, changing and reforming over the tens of thousands of years as it had in the millions that had preceded the coming of man, had been fertile where now it is bare, mountainous where now there are plains and meadows, and legend whispers that in that stark region that is now the Gobi desert, an early, rather primitive civilization existed. The area was not barren then, it was a fertile valley, geological research tells us, and the people thrived. It was here that the breed of canine we know as the Spitz came into being, shaped by those early men through selection from the feral-type dog with whom they had earlier made their pact of friendship.

Within the structure of the tribes that formed this early civilization there were those that were restless, even as there are today in our more highly civilized communities. And these restless ones succumbed to the siren songs of the beckoning hills and left their homes to wander away, to the North, the South, the East and the West, and they took their dogs with them. So there came into being other breeds in other parts of the world, altered to fit their environment, and through selection for certain virtues by man. The Samoyed became a specific breed, the Chow, the Sled Dogs of the North, and the many other breeds that are of the Spitz family, fashioned from the original canine clay, the prototype Spitz.

In this way the qualities of the Spitz tribe spread throughout the world, unmistakably recognizable; the alert expression, the short, prick ears, the sturdiness and quickness, the fluffy tail held high and sometimes over the back; all the tell-tale characteristics of the Spitz family that are to be found in the linking breeds of that family from the tiny, pert Pomeranian to the powerful sled dogs of the far North.

APPEARANCE

The Spitz of today weighs between 16 and 18 pounds. In color he should be solidly white as is the Samoyed. Years ago other colors were permissible as long as they were "self" or solid colors with no mixture of colors or the slightest patch of white on colors other than white. Cream, fawn, brown, and (infrequently) black Spitz were accepted. But today the coat must be pure white, though occasionally a biscuit or light cream is found.

The eyes should be dark brown, the nose, pads, lips, and nails black. Bitches are generally slightly smaller and more delicate than males. The feet should be well knuckled up, the back straight and short so that the body is square. The thighs should be well muscled and the hind legs not over-angulated and should be parallel when standing or moving. The front legs should be parallel and straight with a slight spring in the pastern for flexibility. Shoulders should be long and sloping and the elbow should be tight to the body.

The head of the Spitz is wedge-shaped with rather a sharp muzzle, and the skull should be slightly crowned. The stop should not be too abrupt and the ears must be strong, rather thick, and must ALWAYS be erect. The expression is lively, eager, and cocky.

The coat is a double one with a well developed undercoat. The outer coat stands away from the body forming a ruff around the neck and shoulders which frames the head. The tail is heavily plumed and generally carried over the back.

"PR" Mala Balto, owned by Thomas and Yvonne Houston. Sire: "PR" Stout's Pal Pierre; dam: Frosty the Snow Girl. In this photo it is evident how closely related the Spitz is to the Samoyed, Pomeranian, Keeshond and many of the other Northern breeds.

The gait of the Spitz is a quick, agile, light-footed trot. The dog should move with a free and well-balanced stride with the forequarters easily assimilating the thrust from the strong hindquarters.

The Spitz is a bright, saucy, fascinating breed and very choosy about making friends. Though not a large dog, the Spitz is known for its courage and spunkiness and is ever-ready to repel unwanted advances, by animal or man. Those who are familiar with the breed's character and temperament never take unwanted liberties with this dog of ancient lineage. This typical disposition, combined with its general keenness, makes the Spitz an excellent watchdog. So very attractive in its snowy white coat, black eyes, pert, foxy head, alert ears and perky movement, the Spitz can be purchased at a lower price than most of the other purebred dogs whose breeds are recognized by the A.K.C. Quite frequently, nice specimens of the breed can be found in pet shops and purchased for a nominal sum.

2. Environment

Though of basic northern ancestry, the Spitz has lived with mankind for so many long generations that he has become completely adapted to man's habitat, whether it be in the colder climes which are of the breed's basic heritage, or warmer areas. The Spitz can, and does, live in the deep, hot South, and the cold, far North, and the difference in temperatures seems not to bother him at all.

Dog owners, like so many other people, are prone to shallow thinking, and this leads them to betrayal by their emotions and their love for their pet, which results in a trip to the veterinarian to have their dog's coat clipped close during the summer months. In theory it seems like the proper thing to do. After all, don't we shed our coats in the summer so that we will be comfortable when a wicked, brassy sun permeates the very air with unavoidable and energy-depleting heat particles? Then why not do as much for out pet? Why not remove his heavy coat so that he will be more comfortable?

Look to the South for your answers ... the true South, the desert country of Africa, the Sahara, a place that looks as though it might have been the birthplace of the sun. Through the long ages of man, since before history put names and dates to people, places and events, the inhabitants of the heat-drenched area covered their heads and bodies in many layers of white, flowing robes. This was their protection against the ever present nemesis that glowed sternly above them, the only way they knew to protect the life-needed liquids of their bodies from the thirsty maw of the molten sphere that was their constant enemy.

Take your lesson, then, from them, the people of the desert. The white coat of your Spitz is its protection from the sun and heat. It is insulation, protecting the skin and the moisture of the dog's body. Its very lack of color (generally), the stark whiteness of the white Spitz's coat, is protection, turning the rays of the sun away. The natural shedding process that comes with longer days and the heat they herald has removed enough of the dog's coat to give him comfort in the new, hot season.

Animals that possess pink skin can become sunburned too, if the skin is not protected. This your dog's coat also does, and the skin of a white Spitz is pink so it needs that protection. Having your dog clipped close for the summer also leaves it a prey to the numerous biting flies that come with the hotter seasons.

Frosty Lady, owned by Alice R. DeLestry, is a charming, well-cared-for companion and an ever faithful pet. The proper care of your Spitz will give you endless satisfaction and the pride of possession that comes with owning one of these beautiful dogs.

In other words (if those already used haven't been enough), DON'T have your Spitz's coat clipped off for the summer months. If you wish to help him feel more comfortable when the sun is high and hot, supply him with plenty of fresh, cool drinking water, see that he has a place out of the sun in which to rest (perhaps in the cool cellar), and keep him clean and well-groomed.

EXERCISE

You need not take very special pains to exercise your Spitz. As a breed, and under normal conditions, they are fairly lively and therefore exercising rather constantly. But some formal exercise should be given your Spitz every day. Teach your pet to chase, retrieve and bring back to you a ball or a thrown stick. Give him ten to fifteen minutes of this kind of beneficial exercise. In summertime wait until the sun is down and the cool of evening sets in before you both indulge in this favorite sport. If it is too warm cut the time down or wait until the next day. Also, take your Spitz for nice long walks on the leash. These can be fairly slow walks, in fact the walk can direct you to a park, if you live in the city, where you can give your pet his ball, or stick exercise before returning home.

All this is not only good for your dog, it is good for you, too. You will be getting exercise you wouldn't have gotten if you didn't have a dog, and we, all of us, certainly need any little extra exercise we can possibly get. Playing, walking, finding a rapport with your dog in this manner is also relaxing for you, relieving you of the tensions that have built up during the day and bringing you some measure of quiet repose.

FEEDING

Your Spitz, like all canines, is classified as a carnivore, a flesh eater. His teeth are not made for grinding as are human teeth, they are fashioned for tearing and severing, as are the teeth of his wild relatives the wolves, coyotes, jackals, and wild dogs. The main prey of these wild cousins of your Spitz are the various hoofed herbivorous animals, small animals, and birds, of their native habitat. When the prey is stalked, caught and killed, the carnivores consume the entire body of their prey, beginning usually with the stomach, liver and blood, not just the muscle meat alone. As a matter of fact, the muscle meat is one of the last parts of the animal's body that is eaten, before the bones are cracked and the marrow sucked out.

This diet, that keeps the wild cousins of the dog strong, healthy, and fertile, can do the same for your domesticated pet. Of course in this day and age your dog cannot hunt and live off the land. He depends upon you to supply him with his sustenance and, if you are to supply him well, you must understand what the wild dog gets from his kill and where and how you can find the same elements to feed your Spitz.

The canine hunter first laps the blood of his victim, then tears open the stomach and feeds on the predigested vegetable matter and the fat encrusted intestines. He feasts on liver, kidneys, heart and lungs, tears and consumes the muscle meat, first choosing that which contains the most fat, and finally crushes and consumes the bones, their marrow, and tendons, and connective tissue.

In the process of feasting he has consumed minerals and proteins, vitamins and carbohydrates, fats and fatty acids, roughage for laxation, and from the water he drinks and the sun that shines on him he has been provided with extra minerals and vitamins. To easily purchase and feed to your dog all these elements is the answer to his dietary needs.

BASIC FOODS

Any substance may be considered food if it can be used by an animal as a body-building material, a source of energy, or a regulator of body activity. Your Spitz's diet must be composed of many food materials to provide elements necessary to his growth and health. These necessary ingredients can be purchased in any grocery store. Listed below you will find the dietary essentials and the raw material in which they can be found and that is available to you at the nearest store.

1. PROTEIN: meat, dairy products, eggs, soybeans.
2. FAT: butter, cream, oils, pure animal fat, fatty meat, milk, cream, cheese.
3. CARBOHYDRATES: cereals, vegetables, confectionery syrups, honey.
4. VITAMIN A: greens, peas, beans, asparagus, broccoli, eggs, milk.
5. THIAMINE: vegetables, legumes, whole grains, milk, yeast, organ and muscle meats.
6. RIBOFLAVIN: green leaves, milk, liver, egg yolk, wheat germ, yeast, beef, chicken, cottonseed flour or meal.
7. NIACIN: milk, lean meat, liver, yeast.
8. VITAMIN D: fish that contains oil, fish liver oils, eggs.
9. ASCORBIC ACID: tomatoes, citrus fruits (this element not necessary to feed to dogs).
10. IRON, CALCIUM, AND PHOSPHORUS: milk, vegetables, eggs, soybean, bone marrow, blood, liver, oatmeal.

The first three listed essentials complement each other and compose the basic nutritional needs of your dog. Proteins build new body tissue and are composed of the all-important amino acids. Carbohydrates furnish the fuel for growth and energy; and fat produces heat which becomes energy and enables the dog to store energy against emergency. All the vitamins and minerals, in general, act as regulators of cell activity.

The main objective in combining all these food factors is to mix them in the various amounts necessary to produce a balanced diet. This can be done in a number of ways. Dogs can be fed expensively and they can be fed cheaply, and in each instance they can be fed well. It is the method of feeding that counts, not the cost.

The best way to feed is to select a good manufactured dog food, the grain or pellet type, and begin with this food as the main basis. To it add about 20% fat and milk or meat juices to arrive at the correct mixture. If your dog needs more taste appeal in his food than his diet provides, add some fatty meat, raw or cooked, or any of the canned meats made specifically for dog feeding.

Supply fresh water at all times and never overfeed. If you will examine the label on the manufactured dry food that you buy, you will realize that the manufacturer has anticipated every dietary need of your dog and supplied it in his product. Fat, in quantity enough, would become rancid so this food element you must supply.

SUPPLEMENTS

There are many supplements that can be bought to add to your dog's diet, but they must be used with caution, not because they can do any great harm (unless, in some cases, vast doses are given), but because they are not always necessary. Young puppies, sick animals, animals recovering from ailments, whelping bitches, and bitches that have whelped and cared for large litters, sometimes need special supplements.

When you do find the need to include supplements in your dog's foods, use them sparingly. Follow the directions and do not assume that if a little will do a great deal of good, a lot will be absolutely marvelous. That sort of thinking can lead to disaster. Supplements are composed of vitamins and minerals, and only a very little bit of these substances are needed to have affect upon the recipient.

Incidentally, I do not recommend the feeding of bones to dogs, they can cause too much trouble. Rib bones are sometimes given to dogs by breeders to act as toothbrushes for their dogs. The dog's teeth go through the bone and they are cleaned in the process. The nylon or rawhide bones that are manufactured serve the same purpose with less danger to the dog.

FEEDING TECHNIQUES

The consistency of the food mix can vary to fit the taste of your Spitz. Variety is not necessary. Indeed it can lead to finicky eaters. The dog's nose is so keen that when he lowers his muzzle to the food dish he is able to segregate and take pleasure in all the many and varied ingredients which he scents separately, variety is therefore not necessary.

Keep your feeding utensils clean and try to feed always in the same place and at the same time. In-between-times tidbits are as bad for your dog as they are for you, and will lead to picky eaters and too much weight.

LEADS AND COLLARS

Do not buy a flat collar for your Spitz, it will eventually wear the hair

The Spitz is by nature a hardy animal and what dog people call a "good doer." A sensible diet that includes proper amounts of vitamins, minerals proteins, fats and carbohydrates plus a constant supply of fresh drinking water will keep him in sparkling health for many years.

around the neck and spoil the fine, full mane that is so typical of the breed. A thin, round collar is best, or a light chain link collar of the looped variety that does not buckle. The latter type can hang loose on the dog's neck, and can also be used for training.

If you use a leather collar of any kind, don't forget to clean it whenever you give your dog a bath, or before, if necessary. Often dog owners think that an odor is issuing from the dog when it is the collar that is the culprit. Sebum from the dog's body coats the leather and must be removed. Wash the leather with a good saddle soap, then rinse well and wipe with alcohol. A good leather oil, applied sparingly and worked in, will keep the leather soft and pliable.

Light, strong leads of any material can be used. Many of the leashes are manufactured from nylon and other synthetic materials, and are easy to clean and keep looking well.

SHELTER REQUIREMENTS

Most Spitz pets live in the house with their owners and have their own bed and mattress of wicker or aluminium which can be bought in any pet shop. Or they have a rug in some specific corner which has become their special place and bed. In most instances this is all that is necessary, unless the owner goes to a job and is alone so that the dog is alone all day, too.

When the weather is good it is a shame not to allow your pet to be out in it and able to enjoy it. This is one reason why I advocate a house and run, however small it may be, for your pet. Another reason is if you want to go somewhere and cannot take your dog with you. He is better off outdoors inside a wire run where he can do no harm and no harm can come to him, than allowed to run loose. If the weather changes he can seek shelter in his house and be nice and snug until you come home and bring him inside again.

A house to fit your pet Spitz can be purchased at a pet shop or you can build one yourself if you are at all handy with tools. Make a plan and you can have outdoor plywood cut to your specifications and, with some framing, nail it together. Check costs first. Sometimes you will find that it is cheaper to buy one than attempt to build it. Whether you buy or build make sure that the floor of the house is up off the ground, the roof slopes, and that you have easy access to the inside for the purpose of cleaning. Use oat (or similar) straw for bedding, or cedar shavings which will keep fleas away and impart a nice odor to your dog's coat.

The wire for your run should be sturdy enough to last, and should also be rustproof for the same reason. Sections can be bought that need only be set up, or you can build the run yourself. If you decide on the latter, use either metal or cedar posts for your corners. If cedar, or any other kind of wood, sink them deeply and paint the part that will go underground with creosote to prevent rot. Make and edge all around the run of cement and rocks filling in a dug trench. This will keep your dog from digging out or other dogs from digging in.

One last word of caution; make sure that your run is high enough to keep your dog from jumping over or other dogs from jumping in. If it isn't you defeat the whole purpose of the run.

3. Grooming

Grooming your Spitz is not a difficult job . . . if you do it often enough. If you don't, it will become difficult and an uncomfortable chore for both you and your pet. Regular grooming is particularly necessary when your dog is shedding.

IMPLEMENTS FOR GROOMING

A good wire brush and a metal comb are the most necessary tools for good grooming. Brush away from the lay of the hair, then brush with the hair. Work tangles loose slowly so you will not pull out the guard hair. These are the long hairs that you see. By parting them to the skin you will see the undercoat, shorter, woolier hair, that protects the dog's body from water.

If you do find places where the hair is matted, use the comb to gently work it loose. If you are impatient and abrupt you may tear out some of the guard hair that gives your Spitz such a beautiful coat, and spoil his appearance, for the guard hair takes a long time to grow back fully.

When the dog is shedding extend the time of grooming so that all loose hair is removed from the coat. During shedding some breeders recommend the use of a hacksaw blade as a grooming tool. The teeth are pulled gently through the coat to remove the loose hair.

When you have finished rough grooming brush the mane and tail, and the feathers (hair) on the hind and front legs, up, or away from the body using a little twist of the brush at the end of each stroke. This makes the hair stand up and away in a beautiful halo.

Most people do not realize that it is important to brush a dog out before bathing him. This is the procedure that the owners of all long haired dogs should follow. It is done to release all the sections of coat that may be matted or tangled, for once soaked with water these places become almost impossible to untangle.

BATHING YOUR SPITZ

Make sure you have plenty of towels ready when you are about to bathe your pet. Other necessities are wads of cotton for the ears to keep the water from running into the ear canals. Cotton stick swabs for cleaning the ears. A hair conditioner to remove snarls. A hose spray to attach to the faucet. A toothbrush and baking soda. A blueing type dog shampoo, or any of the many soaps, detergents, foams, etc., that are manufactured solely for dogs. There is even a tearless, lather-type soap for dogs. But, even if you use this latter soap, be careful that you don't get soap in your pet's eyes.

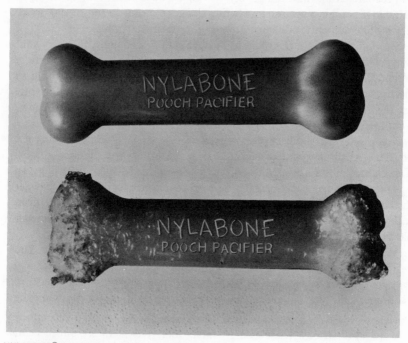

NYLABONE® is a necessity that is available at your local petshop (not in supermarkets). The puppy or grown dog chews the hambone flavored nylon into a frilly dog toothbrush, massaging his gums and cleaning his teeth as he plays. Veterinarians highly recommend this product . . . but beware of cheap imitations which might splinter or break.

If you use the bath tub, or any tub for that matter, and of course you must use one if you are going to bathe your dog, have a rubber mat at the bottom to keep him from slipping.

METHOD OF BATHING

Soak your dog well. Remember that undercoat I mentioned earlier that protects the dog from water? Well you must get through this and to the skin. After the dog is thoroughly soaked apply the soap, first as a collar around the dog's neck, then work down to the hindquarters, rubbing the soap in thoroughly. Then work on the head.

Clean the ears with the cotton swabs, dipping the swabs in alcohol and cleaning out thoroughly. Wet the toothbrush and brush the dog's teeth thoroughly with baking soda. Cleanse them with clean water.

Incidentally, use warm water throughout, never hot water. Work the soap

18

in well with your fingers and hands, massaging thoroughly. When the skin and coat are clean, rinse completely, leaving no trace of the soap or shampoo behind. If you have not used a blueing shampoo, use it in the rinsing water (for a white dog only, of course), to make the coat truly white.

Strip off as much of the water as you can with your hands, then dry your Spitz with the bath towels. If you wish his coat to stand out beautifully around the head or mane) you can "fluff" dry it. To do so you will need an electric hand hair-dryer. Do not dry the mane too thoroughly for fluff drying, use the hand dryer to do this and, as you dry it, brush the hair up and away from the body, "fluffing" it so-to-speak.

If any yellowness still appears after thorough washing and grooming use powdered chalk or powdered magnesia (the latter leaves a pleasant glitter). These same substances can be utilized also as a dry bath for your dog. To use these whiteners, dampen the coat of your Spitz, sprinkle the powder thickly all through the coat. Then keep your dog still until the coat dries with the whitener in it. Lastly brush the coat vigorously until all the whitener has been removed.

All this may sound complicated and time-consuming. Truly it isn't. You will be proud of your glittering white, plumed-tail Spitz; and your dog will be proud, too. They seem to sense the fact that they are well-groomed and handsome and walk in pride and arrogance, lightly spurning the mundane earth.

4. The New Puppy

PREPARING FOR THE PUPPY'S ARRIVAL

Because at least three out of four prospective purchasers of dogs want to buy a young rather than an adult or almost adult dog, the problem of preparing for the arrival of a permanent canine house guest almost always means preparing for the arrival of a puppy. This is not to say that there is anything wrong with purchasing an adult dog; on the contrary, such a purchase has definite advantages in that it often allows freedom from housebreaking chores and rigorous feeding schedules, and these are of definite benefit to prospective purchasers who have little time to spare. Since the great majority of dog buyers, however, prefer to watch their pet grow from sprawlingly playful puppyhood to dignified maturity, buying a dog, practically speaking, means buying a puppy.

Every puppy coming into a new home should have certain items of equipment ready at his arrival. One of these is a comfortable dog bed placed in a corner of his own. Many types of beds are available at your pet shop along with everything else you will need for the new youngster.

Who but the most hard-hearted could resist a delightful ball of living fluff such as this typical Spitz puppy. Such a pet more than makes up for the care he needs in his first year by his matchless devotion and companionship during his lifetime.

Before you get a puppy be sure that you are willing to take the responsibility of training him and caring for his physical needs. His early training is most important, as an adult dog that is a well-behaved member of the family is the end product of your early training. Remember that your new puppy knows only a life of romping with his littermates and the security of being with his mother, and that coming into your home is a new and sometimes frightening experience for him. He will adjust quickly if you are patient with him and show him what you expect of him. If there are small children in the family be sure that they do not abuse him or play roughly with him. A puppy plays hard, but he also requires frequent periods of rest. Before he comes, decide where he is to sleep and where he is to eat. If your puppy does not have a collar, find out the size he requires and buy an inexpensive one, as he will soon outgrow it. Have the proper grooming equipment on hand. Consult the person from whom you bought the puppy as to the proper food for your puppy, and learn the feeding time and amount that he eats a day. Buy him some toys—usually the breeder will give you some particular toy or toys which he has cherished as a puppy to add to his new ones and to make him less homesick. Get everything you need from your pet shop *before* you bring the puppy home.

MALE OR FEMALE?

Before buying your puppy you should have made a decision as to whether you want a male or a female. Unless you want to breed your pet and raise a litter of puppies, your preference as to the sex of your puppy is strictly a personal choice. Both sexes are pretty much the same in disposition and character, and both make equally good pets.

WHERE TO BUY YOUR PUPPY

Although pet shop owners are necessarily restricted from carrying all breeds in stock, they know the best dog breeders and are sometimes able to supply quality puppies on demand. In cases in which a pet shop owner is unable to obtain a dog for you, he can still refer you to a good source, such as a reputable kennel. If your local pet shop proprietor is unable to either obtain a dog for you or refer you to someone from whom you can purchase one, don't give up: there are other avenues to explore. Additional sources of information are the various magazines devoted to the dog fancy.

SIGNS OF GOOD HEALTH

Picking out a healthy, attractive little fellow to join the family circle is a different matter from picking a show dog; it is also a great deal less complicated. Often the puppy will pick you. If he does, and it is mutual admiration at first sight, he is the best puppy for you. At a reliable kennel or pet shop the owner will be glad to answer your questions and to point out the difference between pet and show-quality puppies. Trust your eyes and hands to tell if the puppies are sound in body and temperament. Ears and eyes should not have suspicious discharges. Legs should have strong bones; bodies should have solid muscles. Coats should be clean. Lift the hair to see if the skin is free of scales and parasites.

Temperament can vary from puppy to puppy in the same litter. There is always one puppy which will impress you by his energy and personality. He loves to show off and will fling himself all over you and his littermates, and everyone who comes to see the puppies falls in love with him. However, do not overlook the more reserved puppy. Most dogs are wary of strangers, so reserve may indicate caution, not a timid puppy. He may calmly accept your presence when he senses that all is well. Such a puppy should be a steady reliable dog when mature. In any event, never force yourself on a puppy—let him come to you. Reliable breeders and pet shops will urge you to take your puppy to the veterinarian of your choice to have the puppy's health checked, and will allow you at least two days in which to have it done. It should be clearly understood whether rejection by a veterinarian for health reasons means that you have the choice of another puppy from that litter or that you get your money back.

PAPERS

When you buy a purebred Spitz you should receive his United Kennel Club registration certificate (or an application form to fill out), a pedigree, and a health certificate made out by the breeder's veterinarian. The registration certificate is the official U.K.C. paper. If the puppy was named and registered by his breeder you will want to complete the transfer and send it, with the fee, to the United Kennel Club. They will transfer the dog to your ownership in their records and send a new certificate to you. If you receive, instead, an application for registration, you should fill it out, choosing a name for your dog, and mail it, with the fee, to the U.K.C.

The pedigree is a chart showing your puppy's ancestry and is not a part of his official papers. The health certificate will tell you what shots have been given and when the next ones are due. Your veterinarian will be appreciative of this information, and will continue with the same series of shots if they have not been completed. The health certificate will also give the dates on which the puppy has been wormed. Ask your veterinarian whether rabies shots are required in your locality. Most breeders will give you food for a few days along with instructions for feeding so that your puppy will have the same diet he is accustomed to until you can buy a supply at your petshop.

THE PUPPY'S FIRST NIGHT WITH YOU

The puppy's first night at home is likely to be disturbing to the family. Keep in mind that suddenly being away from his mother, brothers, and sisters is a new experience for him; he may be confused and frightened. If you have a special room in which you have his bed, be sure that there is nothing there with which he can harm himself. Be sure that all lamp cords are out of his reach and that there is nothing that he can tip or pull over. Check furniture that he might get stuck under or behind and objects that he might chew. If you want him to sleep in your room he probably will be quiet all night, reassured by your presence. If left in a room by himself he will cry and howl, and you will have to steel yourself to be impervious to his whining. After a few nights alone he will adjust. The first night that he is alone it is wise to put a loud-ticking alarm clock, as well as his toys, in the room with him. The alarm clock will make a comforting noise, and he will not feel that he is alone.

YOUR PUPPY'S BED

Every dog likes to have a place that is his alone. He holds nothing more sacred than his own bed whether it be a rug, dog crate, or dog bed. If you get your puppy a bed be sure to get one which discourages chewing. Also be sure that the bed is large enough to be comfortable for him when he is fully grown. Locate it away from drafts and radiators. A word might be said here in defense of the crate, which many pet owners think is cruel and confining. Given a choice, a young dog instinctively selects a secure place in which to lounge, rest, or sleep. The walls and ceiling of a crate, even a wire one, answer that need. Once he regards his crate as a safe and reassuring place to stay, you will be able to leave him alone in the house.

FEEDING YOUR PUPPY

As a general rule, a puppy from weaning time (six weeks) to three months of age should have *four meals a day*; from three months to six months, *three meals*; from six months to one year, *two meals*. After a year, a dog does well on *one meal daily*. There are as many feeding schedules as there are breeders, and puppies do fine on all of them, so it is best for the new owner to follow the one given him by the breeder of his puppy. Remember that all dogs are individuals. The amount that will keep your dog in good health is right for him, not the "rule-book" amount. A feeding schedule to give you some idea of what the average puppy will eat is as follows:

Morning meal:	Puppy meal with milk.
Afternoon meal:	Meat mixed with puppy meal, plus a vitamin-mineral supplement.
Evening meal:	Same as afternoon meal, but without a vitamin-mineral supplement.

Do not change the amounts in your puppy's diet too rapidly. If he gets diarrhea it may be that he is eating too much, so cut back on his food and when he is normal again increase his food more slowly.

There is a canned food made especially for puppies which you can buy only by a veterinarian's prescription. Some breeders use this very successfully from weaning to three months.

TRANSITIONAL DIET

Changing over to an adult program of feeding is not difficult. Very often the puppy will change himself; that is, he will refuse to eat some of his meals. He adjusts to his one meal (or two meals) a day without any trouble.

BREAKING TO COLLAR AND LEASH

Puppies are usually broken to a collar before you bring them home, but even if yours has never worn one it is a simple matter to get him used to it. Put a loose collar on him for a few hours at a time. At first he may scratch at it and try to get it off, but gradually he will take it as a matter of course. To break him to a lead, attach his leash to his collar and let him drag it around. When he becomes used to it pick it up and gently pull him in the direction you want him to go. He will think it is a game, and with a bit of patience on your part he will allow himself to be led.

DISCIPLINING YOUR PUPPY

The way to have a well-mannered adult dog is to give him firm basic training while he is a puppy. When you say "*No*" you must mean "*No*." Your dog will respect you only if you are firm. A six- to eight-weeks-old puppy is old enough to understand what "*No*" means. The first time you see your puppy doing something he shouldn't be doing, chewing something he shouldn't chew, or wandering in a forbidden area, it's time to teach him. Shout, "*No*." Puppies do not like loud noises, and your misbehaving pet will readily connect the word with something unpleasant. Usually a firm "*No*" in a disapproving tone of voice is enough to correct your dog, but occasionally you get a puppy that requires a firmer hand, especially as he grows older. In this case hold your puppy firmly and slap him gently across the hindquarters. If this seems cruel, you should realize that no dog resents being disciplined if he is caught in the act of doing something wrong, and your puppy will be intelligent enough to know what the slap was for.

After you have slapped him and you can see that he has learned his lesson, call him to you and talk to him in a pleasant tone of voice—praise him for coming to you. This sounds contradictory, but it works with a puppy. He immediately forgives you, practically tells you that it was his fault and that he deserved his punishment, and promises that it will not happen again. This form of discipline works best and may be used for all misbehaviors.

Never punish your puppy by chasing him around, making occasional swipes with a rolled-up newspaper; punish him only when you have a firm hold on him. Above all, never punish your dog after having called him to you. He must learn to associate coming to you with something pleasant.

HOUSEBREAKING

While housebreaking your puppy do not let him have the run of the house. If you do you will find that he will pick out his own bathroom, which may be in your bedroom or in the middle of the livingroom rug. Keep him confined to a small area where you can watch him, and you will be able to train him much more easily and speedily. A puppy does not want to dirty his bed, but he does need to be taught where he should go. Spread papers over his living quarters, then watch him carefully. When you notice him starting to whimper, sniff the floor, or run agitatedly in little circles, rush him to the place that you want to serve as his relief area and gently hold him there until he relieves himself. Then praise him lavishly. When you remove the soiled papers, leave a small damp piece so that the puppy's sense of smell will lead him back there next time. If he makes a mistake, wash the area at once with warm water, followed by a rinse with water and vinegar or sudsy ammonia. This will kill the odor and prevent discoloration. It shouldn't take more than a few days for him to get the idea of using newspapers. When he becomes fairly consistent, reduce the area of paper to a few sheets in a corner. As soon as you think he has the idea fixed in his mind, you can let him roam around the house a bit, but keep an eye on him. It might be best to keep him on leash the first few days so that you can rush him back to his paper at any signs of an approaching accident.

The normal healthy puppy will want to relieve himself when he wakes up in the morning, after each feeding, and after strenuous exercise. During early puppyhood any excitement, such as the return home of a member of the family or the approach of a visitor, may result in floor-wetting, but that phase should pass in a few weeks. Keep in mind that you can't expect too much from your puppy until he is about five months old. Before that, his muscles and digestive system just aren't under his control.

OUTDOOR HOUSEBREAKING

You can begin outdoor training on leash even while you are paper-training your puppy. First thing in the morning take him outdoors (to the curb, if you are in the city) and walk him back and forth in a small area until he relieves himself. He will probably make a puddle and then walk around, uncertain of what is expected of him. You can try standing him over a newspaper, which may give him the idea. Some dog trainers use glycerine suppositories at this point for fast action. Praise your dog every time taking him outside brings results, and he will get the idea. You'll find, when you begin the outdoor training, that the male puppy usually requires a longer walk than the female. Both male and female puppies will squat. It isn't until he is older that the male dog will begin to lift his leg. If you hate to give up your sleep, you can train your puppy to go outdoors during the day and use the paper at night.

5. Training

WHEN TO START TRAINING

You should never begin SERIOUS obedience training before your dog is seven or eight months old. (Some animal psychologists state that puppies can begin training when seven weeks old, if certain techniques are followed. These techniques, however, are still experimental and should be left to the professional trainer to prove their worth.) While your dog is still in his early puppyhood, concentrate on winning his confidence so he will love and admire you. This will make his training easier, since he will do anything to please you. Basic training can be started at the age of three or four months. He should be taught to walk nicely on a leash, sit and lie down on command, and come when he is called.

YOUR PART IN TRAINING

You must patiently demonstrate to your dog what each word of command means. Guide him with your hands and the training leash, reassuring him with your voice, through whatever routine you are teaching him. Repeat the word associated with the act. Demonstrate again and again to give the dog a chance to make the connection in his mind.

Once he begins to get the idea, use the word of command without any physical guidance. Drill him. When he makes mistakes, correct him, kindly at first, more severely as his training progresses. Try not to lose your patience or become irritated, and never slap him with your hand or the leash during the training session. Withholding praise or rebuking him will make him feel bad enough.

When he does what you want, praise him lavishly with words and with pats. Don't continually reward with dog candy or treats in training. The dog that gets into the habit of performing for a treat will seldom be fully dependable when he can't smell or see one in the offing. When he carries out a command, even though his performance is slow or sloppy, praise him and he will perform more readily the next time.

THE TRAINING VOICE

When you start training your dog, use your training voice, giving commands in a firm, clear tone. Once you give a command, persist until it is obeyed, even if you have to pull the dog to obey you. He must learn that training is different from playing, that a command once given must be obeyed no matter what distractions are present. Remember that the tone and pitch of your voice, not loudness, are the qualities that will influence your dog most.

Be consistent in the use of words during training. Confine your commands to as few words as possible and never change them. It is best for only one person to carry on the dog's training, because different people will use different words and tactics that will confuse your dog. The dog who hears *"come," "get over here," "hurry up," "here, Rex,"* and other commands when he is wanted will become totally confused.

TRAINING LESSONS

Training is hard on the dog—and on the trainer. A young dog just cannot take more than ten minutes of training at a stretch, so limit the length of your first lessons. Then you can gradually increase the length of time to about thirty minutes. You'll find that you too will tend to become impatient when you stretch out a training lesson. If you find yourself losing your temper, stop and resume the lesson at another time. Before and after each lesson have a play period, but don't play during a training session. Even the youngest dog soon learns that schooling is a serious matter; fun comes afterward.

Don't spend too much time on one phase of the training, or the dog will

The remarkable intelligence of the Spitz makes him an excellent pupil in obedience work. Although he can't compete in a trial, he can still learn the lessons and give you the pleasure of owning a model canine citizen.

become bored. Always try to end a lesson on a pleasant note. Actually, in nine cases out of ten, if your dog isn't doing what you want it's because you're not getting the idea over to him properly.

YOUR TRAINING EQUIPMENT AND ITS USE

The leash is more properly called the lead, so we'll use that term here. The best leads for training are the six-foot webbed-cloth leads, usually olive-drab in color, and the six-foot leather lead. Fancier leads are available and may be used if desired.

You'll need a metal-link collar, called a choke chain, consisting of a metal chain with rings on each end. Even though the name may sound frightening, it won't hurt your dog, and it is an absolute MUST in training. There is a right and a wrong way to put the training collar on. It should go around the dog's neck so that you can attach the lead to the ring at the end of the chain which passes OVER, not under his neck. It is most important that the collar is put on properly so it will tighten when the lead is pulled and ease when you relax your grip.

The correct way to hold the lead is also very important, as the collar should have some slack in it at all times, except when correcting. Holding the loop in your right hand, extend your arm to the side, even with your shoulder. With your left hand, grasp the lead as close as possible to the collar, without making it tight. The remaining portion of the lead can be made into a loop which is held in the right hand. Keep this arm close to your body. Most corrections will be made with the left hand by giving the lead a jerk in the direction you want the dog to go. The dog that pulls and forges ahead can be corrected by a steady pull on the lead.

HEELING

"Heeling" in dog language means having your dog walk alongside you on your left side, close to your leg, on lead or off. With patience and effort you can train your dog to walk with you even on a crowded street or in the presence of other dogs.

Now that you have learned the correct way to put on your dog's collar and how to hold the lead, you are ready to start with his first lesson in heeling. Put the dog at your left side, sitting. Using the dog's name and the command *"Heel,"* start forward on your LEFT foot, giving a tug on the lead to get the dog started. Always use the dog's name first, followed by the command, such as *"Rex, heel."* Saying his name will help get his attention and will let him know that you are about to give a command.

Walk briskly, with even steps, going around in a large circle, square, or straight line. While walking, make sure that your dog stays on the left side and close to your leg. If he lags behind, give several tugs on the lead to get him up to you, then praise him for doing well. If he forges ahead or swings wide, stop and jerk the lead sharply and bring him back to the proper position. Always repeat the command when correcting, and praise him when

Your Spitz loves to be with you all the time. For this reason he makes an exemplary traveling companion and should be included in your travel plans whenever it is possible to take him along.

he does well. If your dog continues to pull or lag behind, either your corrections are not severe enough or your timing between correction and praise is off. Do this exercise for only five minutes at first, gradually lengthening it to fifteen, or even half an hour.

To keep your dog's attention, talk to him as you keep him in place. You can also do a series of fast about-turns, giving the lead a jerk as you turn. He will gradually learn that he must pay attention or be jerked to your side. You can vary the routine by changing speeds, doing turns, figure-eights, and by zig-zagging across the training area.

"HEEL" MEANS "SIT," TOO

To the dog, the command *"Heel"* will also mean that he has to sit in the heel position at your left side when you stop walking—with no additional command from you. As you practice heeling, make him sit whenever you stop, at first using the word *"Sit,"* then with no command at all. He'll soon get the idea and sit down when you stop and wait for the command *"Heel"* to start walking again.

TRAINING TO SIT

Training your dog to sit should be fairly easy. Stand him on your left side, holding the lead fairly short, and command him to *"Sit."* As you give the verbal command, pull up slightly with the lead and push his hindquarters down. Do not let him lie down or stand up. Keep him in a sitting position for a moment, then release the pressure on the lead and praise him. Constantly repeat the command as you hold him in a sitting position, thus fitting the word to the action in his mind. After a while he will begin to get the idea and will sit without your having to push his hindquarters down. When he reaches that stage, insist that he sit on command. If he is slow to obey, slap his hindquarters with your hand to get him down fast. *DO NOT HIT HIM HARD!* Teach him to sit on command facing you as well as when he is at your side. When he begins sitting on command with the lead on, try it with the lead off.

THE "LIE DOWN"

The object of this is to get the dog to lie down either on the verbal command *"Down"* or when you give him the hand signal, your hand raised in front of you, palm down. This is one of the most important parts of training. A well-trained dog will drop on command and stay down whatever the temptation: cat-chasing, car-chasing, or another dog across the street.

Don't start training to lie down until the dog is almost letter-perfect in sitting on command. Then place the dog in a sit, and kneel before him. With both hands, reach forward to his legs and take one front leg in each hand, thumbs up, and holding just below his elbows. Lift his legs slightly off the ground and pull them somewhat out in front of him. Simultaneously, give the command *"Down"* and lower his front legs to the ground.

Hold the dog down and stroke him to let him know that staying down is what you want him to do. This method is far better than forcing a young dog down. Using force can cause him to become very frightened and he will begin to dislike any training. Always talk to your dog and let him know that you are very pleased with him, and soon you will find that you have a happy working dog.

After he begins to get the idea, slide the lead under your left foot and give the command *"Down"*. At the same time, pull the lead. This will help get the dog down. Meanwhile, raise your hand in the down signal. Don't expect to accomplish all this in one session. Be patient and work with the dog. He'll cooperate if you show him just what you expect him to do.

THE "STAY"

The next step is to train your dog to stay either in a *"Sit"* or *"Down"* position. Sit him at your side. Give the command *"Stay"* but be careful not to use his name with this command, because hearing his name may lead him to think that some action is expected of him. If he begins to move, repeat *"Stay"* firmly and hold him down in the sit. Constantly repeat the word *"Stay"* to fix the meaning of that command in his mind. After he has learned to stay for a short time, gradually increase the length of his stay. The hand signal for the stay is a downward sweep of your hand toward the dog's nose, with the palm facing him. While he is sitting, walk around him and stand in front of him. Hold the lead at first; later, drop the lead on the ground in front of him and keep him sitting. If he bolts, scold him and place him back in the same position, repeating the command and all the exercise.

Use some word such as *"Okay"* or *"Up"* to let him know when he can get up, and praise him well for a good performance. As this practice continues, walk farther and farther away from him. Later, try sitting him, giving the command to stay, and then walk out of sight, first for a few seconds, then for longer periods. A well-trained dog should stay where you put him without moving until you come and release him.

Similarly, practice having him stay in the down position, first with you near him, later when you step out of sight.

THE "COME" ON COMMAND

You can train your dog to come when you call him, if you begin when he is young. At first, work with him on lead. Sit the dog, then back away the length of the lead and call him, putting into your voice as much coaxing affection as possible. Give an easy tug on the lead to get him started. When he does come, make a big fuss over him; it might help at this point to give him a small piece of dog candy or food as a reward. He should get the idea soon. You can also move away from him the full length of the lead and call to him something like *"Rex, come,"* then run backward a few steps and stop, making him sit directly in front of you.

For the many years that the Spitz has been the companion of man, he has proven adaptable to any role his masters wished for him. Today the Spitz embodies these same qualities, and they stand him in good stead to make him one of the finest pet dogs to be had anywhere.

Don't be too eager to practice coming on command off lead. Wait until you are certain that you have the dog under perfect control before you try calling him when he's free. Once he gets the idea that he can disobey a command and get away with it, your training program will suffer a serious setback. Keep in mind that your dog's life may depend on his immediate response to a command to come when he is called. If he disobeys off lead, put the lead back on and correct him severely with jerks of the lead.

TEACHING TO COME TO HEEL

The object of this is for you to stand still, say *"Heel,"* and have your dog come right over to you and sit by your left knee in the heel position. If your dog has been trained to sit without command every time you stop, he's ready for this step.

Sit him in front of and facing you and step back one step. Moving only your left foot, pull the dog behind you, then step forward and pull him around until he is in a heel position. You can also have the dog go around by passing the lead behind your back. Use your left heel to straighten him out if he begins to sit behind you or crookedly. This may take a little work, but he will get the idea if you show him just what you want.

THE "STAND"

Your dog should be trained to stand in one spot without moving his feet, and he should allow a stranger to run his hand over his body and legs without showing any resentment or fear. Employ the same method you used in training him to stay on the sit and down. While walking, place your left hand out, palm toward his nose, and command him to stay. His first impulse will be to sit, so be prepared to stop him by placing your hand under his body, near his hindquarters, and holding him until he gets the idea that this is different from the command to sit. Praise him for standing, then walk to the end of the lead. Correct him strongly if he starts to move. Have a stranger approach him and run his hands over the dog's back and down his legs. Keep him standing until you come back to him. Walk around him from his left side, come to the heel position, and make sure that he does not sit until you command him to.

This is a very valuable exercise. If you plan to show your dog he will have learned to stand in a show pose and will allow the judge to examine him.

TRAINING SCHOOLS AND CLASSES

There are dog-training classes in all parts of the country, some sponsored by the local humane society.

If you feel that you lack the time or the skill to train your dog yourself, there are professional dog trainers who will do it for you, but basically dog training is a matter of training YOU and your dog to work together as a team, and if you don't do it yourself you will miss a lot of fun. Don't give up after trying unsuccessfully for a short time. Try a little harder and you and your dog will be able to work things out.

6. Breeding

THE QUESTION OF SPAYING

If you feel that you will never want to raise a litter of purebred puppies, and if you do not wish to risk the possibility of an undesirable mating and surplus mongrel puppies inevitably destined for execution at the local pound, you may want to have your female spayed. Spaying is generally best performed after the female has passed her first heat and before her first birthday: this allows the female to attain the normal female characteristics, while still being young enough to avoid the possible complications encountered when an older female is spayed. A spayed female will remain a healthy, lively pet. You often hear that an altered female will become very fat. However, if you cut down on her food intake, she will not gain weight.

On the other hand, if you wish to enjoy the excitement and feeling of accomplishment of breeding and raising a litter of puppies, particularly in your breed and from your pet, then definitely do not spay.

Male dogs, unlike tomcats, are almost never altered (castrated).

SEXUAL PHYSIOLOGY

Females usually reach sexual maturity (indicated by the first heat cycle, or season) at eight or nine months of age, but sexual maturity may occur as early as six months or as late as thirteen months of age. The average heat cycle (estrus period) lasts for twenty or twenty-one days, and occurs approximately every six months. For about five days immediately preceding the heat period, the female generally displays restlessness and an increased appetite. The vulva, or external genitals, begin to swell. The discharge, which is bright red at the onset and gradually becomes pale pink to straw in color, increases in quantity for several days and then slowly subsides, finally ceasing altogether. The vaginal discharge is subject to much variation: in some bitches it is quite heavy, in others it may never appear, and in some it may be so slight as to go unnoticed.

About eight or nine days after the first appearance of the discharge, the female becomes very playful with other dogs, but will not allow a mating to take place. Anywhere from the tenth or eleventh day, when the discharge has virtually ended and the vulva has softened, to the seventeenth or eighteenth day, the female will accept males and be able to conceive. Many biologists apply the term "heat" only to this receptive phase rather than to the whole estrus, as is commonly done by dog fanciers.

With the proper introduction the Spitz will readily adapt himself to other pets in the household. While he craves the attention of his human family he can be made to understand that it is necessary to share with other animals if the situation demands this.

The young puppy depends on his owner, not only for the basic creature comforts he must have, but also for the direction and guidance that will make the lovable puppy into a fine, dignified adult that brings pride to his owner and credit to every member of his breed.

The ova (egg cells) from the female's ovaries are discharged into the oviduct toward the close of the acceptance phase, usually from the sixteenth to eighteenth day. From the eighteenth day until the end of the cycle, the female is still attractive to males, but she will repulse their advances. The entire estrus, however, may be quite variable: in some females vaginal bleeding ends and mating begins on the fourth day; in others, the discharge may continue throughout the entire cycle and the female will not accept males until the seventeenth day or even later.

The male dog—simply referred to by fanciers as the "dog," in contrast to the female, which is referred to as the "bitch"—upon reaching sexual maturity, usually at about six to eight months, is able, like other domesticated mammals, to breed at any time throughout the year.

The testes, the sperm-producing organs of the male, descend from the body cavity into the scrotum at birth. The condition of *cryptorchidism* refers to the retention of one or both testes within the body cavity. A testicle retained within the body cavity is in an environment too hot for it to function normally. A retained testicle may also become cancerous. If only

Very often a young puppy will come into a new home with no previous experience on a lead. Patience and kindness will go a long way in teaching the clever Spitz puppy proper manners in the all-important matter of good lead manners.

one testicle descends, the dog is known as a *monorchid*; if neither descends, the dog is known as an *anorchid* (dog fanciers, however, refer to a dog with the latter condition as a cryptorchid). A monorchid dog is a fertile animal; and anorchid is sterile.

The male dog's penis has a bulbous enlargement at its base and, in addition, like the penis of a number of other mammals, contains a bone. When mating occurs, pressure on the penis causes a reflex action that fills the bulb with blood, swelling it to about five times its normal size within the female. This locks, or ties, the two animals together. After ejaculation, the animals usually remain tied for fifteen to thirty minutes, but they may separate very quickly or remain together an hour or more, depending on the length of time it takes for the blood to drain from the bulb.

CARE OF THE FEMALE IN ESTRUS

If you have a dog-proof run within your yard, it will be safe to leave your female in season there; if you don't have such a run, she should be shut indoors. Don't leave her alone outside even for a minute: she should be exercised only on lead. If you want to prevent the neighborhood dogs from congregating around your doorstep, as they inevitably will as soon as they discover that your female is in season, take her some distance from the house before you let her relieve herself. Take her in your car to a park or field for a chance to "stretch" her legs (always on lead of course). Keep watch for male dogs, and if one approaches take the female back to the car. After the three weeks are up you can let her out as before with no worry that she can have puppies until her next season.

Some owners find it simpler to board their female at a kennel until her season is over. However, it really is not difficult to watch your female at home. There are various products on the market which are useful at this time. Although the female in season keeps herself quite clean, sometimes she unavoidably stains furniture or rugs. You can buy sanitary belts made especially for dogs at your pet shop. Consult your veterinarian for information on pills to be taken to check odor during this period. There also is a pill that prevents the female from coming in season for extended periods, and there are many different types of liquids, powders, and sprays of varying efficiency used to keep male dogs away. However, the one safe rule (whatever products you use) is: keep your bitch away from dogs that could mount her.

SHOULD YOU BREED YOUR MALE?

As with every question, whether or not to use a male dog as a stud has two sides. The arguments for and against using a dog as a stud are often very close to the ridiculous. A classic example would be the tale that once you use a dog as a stud he will lose his value as a house dog or any one of the other functions a dog may have.

SHOULD YOU BREED YOUR FEMALE?

If you are an amateur and decide to breed your female it would be wise to talk with a breeder and find out all that breeding and caring for puppies entails. You must be prepared to assume the responsibility of caring for the mother through her pregnancy and for the puppies until they are of saleable age. Raising a litter of puppies can be a rewarding experience, but it means work as well as fun, and there is no guarantee of financial profit. As the puppies grow older and require more room and care, the amateur breeder, in desperation, often sells the puppies for much less than they are worth; sometimes he has to give them away. If the cost of keeping the puppies will drain your finances, think twice.

If you have given careful consideration to all these things and still want to breed your female, remember that there is some preparation necessary before taking this step.

WHEN TO BREED

It is usually best to breed in the second or third season. Consider when the puppies will be born and whether their birth and later care will interfere with your work or vacation plans. Gestation period is approximately fifty-eight to sixty-three days. Allow enough time to select the right stud for her. Don't be in a position of having to settle for any available male if she comes into season sooner than expected. Your female will probably be ready to breed twelve days after the first colored discharge. You can usually make arrangements to board her with the owner of the male for a few days to insure her being there at the proper time, or you can take her to be mated and bring her home the same day. If she still appears receptive she may be bred again a day or two later. Some females never show signs of willingness, so it helps to have the experience of a breeder. The second day after the discharge changes color is the proper time; she may be bred for about three days following. For an additional week or so she may have some discharge and attract other dogs by her odor, but she can seldom be bred at this time.

HOW TO SELECT A STUD

Choose a mate for your female with an eye to countering her deficiencies. If possible, both male and female should have several ancestors in common within the last two or three generations, as such combinations generally "click" best. The male should have a good record as a producer. The owner of the stud usually charges a fee for the use of the dog. The fee varies. Payment of a fee does not guarantee a litter, but it does generally confer the right to breed your female again to the stud if she does not have puppies the first time. In some cases the owner of the stud will agree to take a choice puppy in place of a stud fee. You and the owner of the stud should settle all details beforehand, including such questions as what age the puppies should reach before the stud's owner can make his choice, what disposition is made of a single surviving puppy under an agreement by which the stud owner has pick of the litter, and so on. In all cases it is best that the agreement entered into by bitch owner and stud owner be in the form of a written contract.

PREPARATION FOR BREEDING

Before you breed your female, make sure she is in good health. She should be neither too thin nor too fat. Skin diseases must be cured before breeding; a bitch with skin diseases can pass them on to her puppies. If she has worms she should be wormed before being bred, or within three weeks afterwards. It is a good idea to have your veterinarian give her a booster shot for distemper and hepatitis before the puppies are born. This will increase the immunity the puppies receive during their early, most vulnerable period. Choose a dependable veterinarian and rely on him if there is an emergency when your female whelps.

HOW OFTEN SHOULD YOU BREED YOUR FEMALE?

Do not breed your bitch after she reaches six years of age. If you wish to breed her several times while she is young, it is wise to breed her only once a year. In other words, breed her, skip a season, and then breed her again. This will allow her to gain back her full strength between whelpings.

Every breeding should be done with specific goals in mind. The improvement of the breed and the production of puppies that will bring joy to their new owners should be the two main aims of those that have taken the responsibility for the future generations of the breed.

A Spitz mother will often join in the games of her little ones. There is more than play involved here though. It is during these sessions that she teaches her puppies something of the world they will be going into and how to deal with situations encountered in every day life.

The owner of a Spitz puppy is advised to take weekly weight checks on his pet. Steady weight gain is a good pointer to proper condition and a fairly reliable barometer of general health.

THE IMPORTANCE AND APPLICATION OF GENETICS

Any person attempting to breed dogs should have a basic understanding of the transmission of traits, or characteristics, from the parents to the off-spring and some familiarity with the more widely used genetic terms that he will probably encounter. A knowledge of the fundamental mechanics of genetics enables a breeder to better comprehend the passing, complementing, and covering of both good points and faults from generation to generation. It enables him to make a more judicial and scientific decision in selecting potential mates.

Inheritance, fundamentally, is due to the existence of microscopic units, known as *GENES,* present in the cells of all individuals. Genes somehow control the biochemical reactions that occur within the embryo or adult organism. This control results in changing or guiding the development of the organism's characteristics. A "string" of attached genes is known as a *CHROMOSOME.* With a few important exceptions, every chromosome has a partner chromosome carrying a duplicate or equivalent set of genes. Each gene, therefore, has a partner gene, known as an *ALLELE.* The number of different pairs of chromosomes present in the cells of the organism varies with the type of organism: a certain parasitic worm has only one pair, a certain fruit fly has four different pairs, man has 23 different pairs, and your dog has 39 different pairs per cell. Because each chromosome may have many hundreds of genes, a single cell of the body may contain a total of several thousand genes. Heredity is obviously a very complex matter.

In the simplest form of genetic inheritance, one particular gene and its duplicate, or allele, on the partner chromosome control a single characteristic. The presence of freckles in the human skin, for example, is believed to be due to the influence of a single pair of genes.

Each cell of the body contains the specific number of paired chromosomes characteristic of the organism. Because each type of gene is present on both chromosomes of a chromosome pair, *each type of gene is therefore present in duplicate.* The fusion of a sperm cell from the male with an egg cell from the female, as occurs in fertilization, should therefore result in offspring having a *quadruplicate number* (4) of each type of gene. Mating of these individuals would then produce progeny having an *octuplicate number* (8) of each type of gene, and so on. This, however, is normally prevented by a special process. When ordinary body cells prepare to divide to form more tissue, each pair of chromosomes duplicates itself so that there are four partner chromosomes of each kind instead of only two. When the cell divides, two of the four partners, or one pair, go into each new cell. This process, known as *MITOSIS,* insures that each new body cell contains the proper number of chromosomes. Reproductive cells (sperm cell and egg cells), however, undergo a special kind of division known as *MEIOSIS.* In meiosis, the chromosome pairs do *not* duplicate

42

themselves, and thus when the reproductive cells reach the final dividing stage only one chromosome, or one half of the pair, goes into each new reproductive cell. Each reproductive cell, therefore, has only half the normal number of chromosomes. These are referred to as *HAPLOID* cells, in contrast to *DIPLOID* cells, which have the full number of chromosomes. When the haploid sperm cell fuses with the haploid egg cell in fertilization, the resulting offspring has the normal diploid number of chromosomes.

If both partner genes, or alleles, affect the trait in an identical manner, the genes are said to be *HOMOZYGOUS,* but if one affects the character in a manner different from the other gene, or allele, the genes are said to be *HETEROZYGOUS.* For example, in the pair of genes affecting eye color in humans, if each gene of the pair produces blue eyes, the genes (and also the person carrying the genes) are said to be homozygous for blue eyes. If, however, one gene of the pair produces blue eyes, while the other gene, or allele, produces brown eyes, they are said to be heterozygous. The presence of heterozygous genes raises the question, *"Will the offspring have blue eyes or brown eyes?"* which in turn introduces another genetic principle: *DOMINANCE* and *RECESSIVENESS.*

If one gene of a pair can block the action of its partner, or allele, while still producing its own affect, that gene is said to be *dominant* over its allele. Its allele, on the other hand, is said to be recessive. In the case of heterozygous genes for eye color, the brown eye gene is dominant over the recessive blue eye gene, and the offspring therefore will have brown eyes. Much less common is the occurrence of gene pairs in which neither gene is completely dominant over the other. This, known as *INCOMPLETE* or *PARTIAL DOMINANCE,* results in a blending of the opposing influences. In cattle, if a homozygous (pure) red bull is mated with a homozygous (pure) white cow, the calf will be roan, a blending of red and white hairs in its coat, rather than either all red or all white.

During meiosis, or division of the reproductive (sperm and egg) cells, each pair of chromosomes splits, and one-half of each pair goes into one of the two new cells. Thus, in the case of eye color genes, one new reproductive cell will get the chromosome carrying the blue eye gene, while the other new reproductive cell will get the chromosome carrying the brown eye gene, and so on for each pair of chromosomes. If an organism has only two pairs of chromosomes—called pair A, made up of chromosomes A_1 and A_2, and pair B, made up of chromosomes B_1 and B_2—each new reproductive cell will get one chromosome, from each pair and four different combinations are possible. A_1 and B_1; A_1 and B_2; A_2 and B_1, or A_2 and B_2. If the blue eye gene is on A_1, the brown eye gene on A_2, the gene for curly hair on B_1 and the gene for straight hair on B_2, each of the above combinations will exert a different genetic effect on the offspring. This different grouping of chromosomes in the new reproductive cell as a result of meiotic

Breeding animals should be selected for their closeness to breed type, general health, temperament and vigor. Such a typical Spitz as this one would, doubtless, make a fine producer.

cell division is known as *INDEPENDENT ASSORTMENT* and is one reason why variation occurs in the offspring. In the dog, with 39 pairs of chromosomes, the possibilities of variation through independent assortment are tremendous.

But variation does not end here. For example, if two dominant genes, such as the genes for brown eyes and dark hair, were on the same chromosome, all brown-eyed people would have dark hair. Yet in instances where such joined or *LINKED* genes do occur, the two characteristics do not always appear together in the same offspring. This is due to a process known as *CROSS-OVER* or *RECOMBINATION*. Recombination is the mutual exchange of corresponding blocks of genes between the two chromosomes in a pair. That is, during cell division, the two chromosomes may exchange their tip sections or other corresponding segments. If the segments exchanged contain the eye color genes, the brown eye gene will be transferred from the chromosome carrying the dark hair gene to the chromosome carrying the light hair gene, and then brown eyes will occur with light hair, provided that the individual is homozygous for the recessive light hair gene.

Normal Spitz puppies are alert, curious animals. They show neither fear nor animosity when meeting new animals and people for the first time, and proper training will keep them that way.

Due to genetic influence two individuals in a litter may be very much alike or entirely different in matters of conformation and temperament.

Another important source of variation is *MUTATION*. In mutation, a gene becomes altered, such as by exposure to irradiation, and exerts a different effect than it did before. Most mutations are harmful to the organism, and some may result in death. Offspring carrying mutated genes and showing the effects of these mutations are known as *MUTANTS* or *SPORTS*. Mutation also means that instead of only two alleles for eye color, such as brown and blue, there may now be three or more (gray, black, etc.) creating a much larger source for possible variation in the off-spring.

Further complications in the transmission and appearance of genetic traits are the phenomena known as *EPISTASIS* and *PLEIOTROPY*. Epistasis refers to a gene exerting influence on genes other than its own allele. In all-white red-eyed (albino) guinea pigs, for example, the gene controlling intensity of color is epistatic to any other color gene and prevents that gene from producing its effect. Thus, even if a gene for red spots were present in the cells of the guinea pig, the color intensity gene would prevent the red spots from appearing in the guinea pig's white coat. *Pleiotropy* refers to the fact that a single gene may control a number of characteristics. In the fruit fly, for example, the gene that controls eye color may also affect the structure of certain body parts and even the lifespan of the insect.

The puppy's individual characteristics are determined by the germ plasm of his parents, not what they were themselves. This is why a fine dog may not be a top producer and a dog of lesser individual worth can be counted on for litter after litter of typical animals embodying everything wanted in the breed.

One special pair of chromosomes is known as the sex chromosomes. In man, dog, and other mammals, these chromosomes are of two types, designated as X and Y. Under normal conditions, a mammal carrying two X-type sex chromosomes is a female, whereas a mammal carrying one X-type and one Y-type is a male. Females, therefore, have only X chromosomes and can only contribute X chromosomes to the offspring, but the male may contribute either an X or a Y.

If the male's sperm carrying an X chromosome fertilizes the female's egg cell (X), the offspring (XX) will be female; if a sperm carrying a Y chromosome fertilizes the egg (X), the offspring (XY) will be male. It is the male, therefore, that determines the sex of the offspring in mammals.

Traits controlled by genes present on the sex chromosome, and which appear in only one sex, are said to be *SEX LINKED*. If, for example, a rare recessive gene occurs on the X chromosome, it cannot exert its effect in the female because the dominant allele on the other X chromosome will counteract it. In the male, however, there is no second X chromosome, and if the Y chromosome cannot offer any countereffect, the recessive character will appear. There are also *SEX-LIMITED* characteristics: these appear primarily or solely in one sex, but the genes for these traits are not carried on the sex chromosomes. Sex-limited traits appear when genes on other chromosomes exert their effect in the proper hormonal (male or female) environment. Sex-linked and sex-limited transmission is how a trait may skip a generation, by being passed from grandfather to grandson through a mother in which the trait, though present, does not show.

In dealing with the simplest form of heredity—one gene effecting one character—there is an expected ratio of the offspring displaying the character to those who do not display it, depending upon the genetic makeup of the parents. If a parent is homozygous for a character, such as blue eyes, it makes no difference which half of the chromosome pair enters the new reproductive cell, because each chromosome carries the gene for blue eyes. If a parent is heterozygous, however, one reproductive cell will receive the brown eye gene while the other will receive the blue eye gene. If both parents are homozygous for blue eyes, all the offspring will receive two blue eye genes, and all will have blue eyes. If a parent is homozygous for blue eyes, and the other parent is homozygous for brown eyes, all the offspring will be heterozygous, receiving one brown eye gene and one blue eye gene, and because brown is dominant, all will have brown eyes. If both parents are heterozygous, both the blue eye gene and the brown eye gene from one parent have an equal likelihood of ending up with the either blue eye or the brown eye gene from the other parent. This results in a ratio of two heterozygous offspring to the one homozygous for brown eyes and one homozygous for blue eyes, giving a total genetic, or genotypic, ratio of 2:1:1 or, as it is more commonly arranged, 1:2:1. As the two heterozygous as well as the homozygous brown eye offspring will have brown eyes, the ratio of brown eyes to blue eyes (or phenotypic ratio) will be 3:1.

If one parent is heterozygous and the other parent is homozygous for the recessive gene for blue eyes, half of the offspring will be homozygous for blue eyes and will have blue eyes, but the other half of the offspring will be heterozygous and have brown eyes. (Here both the genotypic and phenotypic ratio is 1:1.)

If the homozygous parent, however, has the dominant gene (brown eyes), half of the offspring will be heterozygous and half will be homozygous, as before, but all will have brown eyes. By repeated determinations of these ratios in the offspring, geneticists are able to analyze the genetic makeup of the parents.

Before leaving heredity, it might be well to explain the difference

Although your new Spitz puppy is naturally bright, his learning processes will be materially helped if he is kept to the same routine of feeding, rest and exercise every day.

Most puppies will nurse from their mother for the first three to five weeks of their lives. A good mother will allow her litter to nurse until they can be started on supplementary feeding.

Once introduced to solid food, Spitz puppies can be weaned quite rapidly. If the litter is healthy and puppies have good appetites they will adapt readily to a meat diet.

The wise breeder knows that if all is normal with the dam there is no hurry to wean her puppies off her. The mother's milk is the best diet these infants can have, and the lessons they learn from their dam will be valuable throughout their lives.

between inbreeding, outcrossing, line breeding, and similar terms. Basically, there are only inbreeding and outbreeding. Inbreeding, however, according to its intensity, is usually divided into inbreeding proper and line breeding. Inbreeding proper is considered to be the mating of very closely related individuals, generally within the immediate family, but this is sometimes extended to include matings to first cousins and grandparents. Line breeding is the mating of more distantly related animals, that is, animals, not immediately related to each other but having a common ancestor, such as the same grandsire or great-grandsire. Outbreeding is divided into outcrossing, which is the mating of dogs from different families within the same breed, and cross-breeding, which is mating purebred dogs from different breeds.

From the foregoing discussion of genetics, it should be realized that the theory of telegony, which states that the sire of one litter can influence future litters sired by other studs, is simply not true; it is possible, however, if several males mate with a female during a single estrus cycle, that the various puppies in the litter may have different sires (but not two sires for any one puppy). It should also be realized that blood does not really enter into the transmission of inheritance, although people commonly speak of "bloodlines," "pure-blooded," etc.

7. Care of the Mother and Family

PRENATAL CARE OF THE FEMALE

You can expect the puppies nine weeks from the day of breeding, although 58 days is as common as 63. During this time the female should receive normal care and exercise. If she is overweight, don't increase her food at first; excess weight at whelping time is not good. If she is on the thin side, build her up, giving her a morning meal of cereal and egg yolk. Consult your veterinarian as to increasing her vitamins and mineral supplement. During the last weeks the puppies grow enormously, and the mother will have little room for food and less appetite. Divide her meals into smaller portions and feed her more often. If she loses her appetite, tempt her with meat, liver, chicken, etc.

As she grows heavier, eliminate violent exercise and jumping. Do not eliminate exercise entirely, as walking is beneficial to the female in whelp, and mild exercise will maintain her muscle tone in preparation for the birth. Weigh your female after breeding and keep a record of her weight each week thereafter. Groom your bitch daily—some females have a slight discharge during gestation, more prevalent during the last two weeks, so wash the vulva with warm water daily. Usually, by the end of the fifth week you can notice a broadening across her loins, and her breasts become firmer. By the end of the sixth week your veterinarian can tell you whether or not she is pregnant.

PREPARATION OF WHELPING QUARTERS

Prepare a whelping box at least a week before the puppies are to arrive and allow the mother-to-be to sleep there overnight or to spend some time in it during the day to become accustomed to it. She is then less likely to try to have her litter under the front porch or in the middle of your bed.

The box should have a wooden floor. Sides should be high enough to keep the puppies in but low enough to allow the mother to get out after she has fed them. Layers of newspapers spread over the whole area will make excellent bedding and will be absorbent enough to keep the surface warm and dry. They should be removed when wet or soiled and replaced with another thick layer. An old quilt or blanket is more comfortable for the mother and makes better footing for the nursing puppies, at least during the first week, than slippery newspaper. The quilt should be secured firmly.

SUPPLIES TO HAVE ON HAND

As soon as you have the whelping box prepared, set up the nursery by

The breeder's greatest pride is in the plump, appealing puppies that he can make available to those seeking a fine, pet Spitz. The well-bred, well-started Spitz will assure the buyer's continued satisfaction.

collecting the various supplies you will need when the puppies arrive. You should have the following items on hand: a box lined with towels for the puppies, a heating pad or hot water bottle to keep the puppy box warm, a pile of clean terrycloth towels or washcloths to remove membranes and to dry puppies, a stack of folded newspapers, a roll of paper towels, vaseline, rubber gloves, soap, iodine, muzzle, cotton balls, a small pair of blunt scissors to cut umbilical cords (stick them into an open bottle of alcohol so they keep freshly sterilized), a rectal thermometer, white thread, a flashlight in case the electricity goes off, a waste container, and a scale for weighing each puppy at birth.

It is necessary that the whelping room be warm and free from drafts, because puppies are delivered wet from the mother. Keep a little notebook and pencil handy so you can record the duration of the first labor and the time between the arrival of each puppy. If there is trouble in whelping, this is the information that the veterinarian will want. Keep his telephone number handy in case you have to call him in an emergency, and warn him to be prepared for an emergency, should you need him.

When buying a puppy there are certain papers that the breeder, or seller, should provide the new owner with. A pedigree, a registration certificate, or application, and some information on the puppy's medical history and care should go with every puppy leaving to a new home.

While he is nursing, the puppy is protected from disease by natural antibodies in his mother's milk. After he is weaned he should be put on a regular schedule of temporary inoculations until he is old enough for a permanent shot.

WHELPING

Be prepared for the actual whelping several days in advance. Usually the female will tear up papers, try to dig nests, refuse food, and generally act restless and nervous. These may be false alarms; the real test is her temperature, which will drop to below 100° about twelve hours before whelping. Take her temperature rectally at a set time each day, starting about a week before she is due to whelp. After her temperature goes down, keep her constantly with you or put her in the whelping box and stay in the room with her. She will seem anxious and look to you for reassurance. Be prepared to remove the membranes covering the puppy's head if the mother fails to do this, for the puppy could smother otherwise.

The mother should start licking the puppy as soon as it is out of the sac, thus drying and stimulating it, but if she does not perform this task you can do it with a soft rough towel, instead. The afterbirth should follow the birth of each puppy, attached to the puppy by the umbilical cord. Watch to make sure that each is expelled, for retaining this material can cause infection. The mother probably will eat the afterbirth after biting the cord. One or two will not hurt her; they stimulate the milk supply as well as labor for remaining puppies. Too many, however, can make her lose her appetite for the food she needs to feed her puppies and regain her strength, so remove the rest of them along with the soiled newspapers, and keep the box dry and clean to relieve her anxiety.

If a puppy does not start breathing, wrap him in a towel, hold him upside down with his head toward the ground, and shake him vigorously. If he still does not breathe, rub his ribs briskly; if this also fails, administer artificial respiration by compressing the ribs about twenty times per minute.

If the mother does not bite the cord, or bites it too close to the body, you should take over the job to prevent an umbilical hernia. Cut the cord a short distance from the body with your blunt scissors. Put a drop of iodine on the end of the cord; it will dry up and fall off in a few days.

The puppies should follow each other at regular intervals, but deliveries can be as short as five minutes or as long as two hours apart. A puppy may be presented backwards; if the mother does not seem to be in trouble, do not interfere. But if enough of the puppy is outside the birth canal, use a rough towel and help her by pulling gently on the puppy. Pull only when she pushes. A rear-first, or breech, birth can cause a puppy to strangle on its own umbilical cord, so don't let the mother struggle too long. Breech birth is quite common.

When you think all the puppies have been whelped, have your veterinarian examine the mother to determine if all the afterbirths have been expelled. He will probably give her an injection to be certain that the uterus is clean, a shot of calcium for prevention of eclampsia, and possibly an injection of penicillin to prevent infection.

54

RAISING THE PUPPIES

Hold each puppy to a breast as soon as you have dried him. This will be an opportunity to have a good meal without competition. Then place him in the small box that you have prepared so he will be out of his mother's way while she is whelping. Keep a record of birth weights and take weekly readings thereafter so that you will have an accurate account of the puppies' growth. After the puppies have arrived, take the mother outside for a walk and a drink, and then leave her to take care of them. Offer her a dish of vanilla ice cream or milk with corn syrup in it. She usually will eat lying down while the puppies are nursing and will appreciate the coolness of the ice cream during warm weather or in a hot room. She will not want to stay away from her puppies more than a minute or two the first few weeks. Be sure to keep water available at all times, and feed her milk or broth frequently, as she needs liquids to produce milk. To encourage her to eat, offer her the foods she likes best, until she "asks" to be fed without your tempting her. She will soon develop a ravenous appetite and should be fed whenever she is hungry.

Be sure that all the puppies are getting enough to eat. Cut their claws with special dog "nail" clippers, as they grow rapidly and scratch the mother as the puppies nurse. Normally the puppies should be completely weaned by six weeks, although you may start to give them supplementary feedings at three weeks. They will find it easier to lap semi-solid food.

As the puppies grow up, the mother will go into the box only to nurse them, first sitting up and then standing. To dry up her milk supply completely, keep her away from her puppies for longer periods. After a few days of part-time nursing she will be able to stay away for much longer periods of time, and then completely. The little milk left will be resorbed.

When the puppies are five weeks old, consult your veterinarian about temporary shots to protect them against distemper and hepatitis; it is quite possible for dangerous infectious germs to reach them even though you keep their living quarters sanitary. You can expect the puppies to need at least one worming before they are ready to go to their new homes, so take a stool sample to your veterinarian before they are three weeks old. If one puppy has worms, all should be wormed. Follow your veterinarian's advice.

The puppies may be put outside, unless it is too cold, as soon as their eyes are open (about ten days), and they will benefit from the sunlight. A rubber mat or newspapers underneath their box will protect them from cold or dampness.

HOW TO TAKE CARE OF A LARGE LITTER

The size of a litter varies greatly. If your bitch has a large litter she may have trouble feeding all of the puppies. You can help her by preparing

When there are small children in a family they should be made to understand that the puppy is a baby, and must be treated with kindness. Youngsters should not be allowed to tease a small puppy or disturb it during meals or naps.

Recent studies by animals behaviorists have revealed that the first twelve weeks of a puppy's life are most vital to his character development. It is in this period that his attitude toward his canine peers and human acquaintances is formed.

Learning to eat by himself is an important lesson for a young puppy. Supplementary feeding should start with warmed evaporated milk mixed with water. This should be followed by offering baby cereal or puppy meal. Only after he is eating the meal normally should meat be introduced into his diet.

an extra puppy box. Leave half the litter with the mother and the other half in a warm place, changing their places at two-hour intervals at first. Later you may change them less frequently, leaving them all together except during the day. Try supplementary feeding, too, as soon as their eyes are open.

CAESAREAN SECTION

If your female goes into hard labor and is not able to give birth within two hours, you will know that there is something wrong. Call your veterinarian for advice. Some females must have Caesarean sections (taking puppies from the mother by surgery), but don't be alarmed if your dog has to undergo this. The operation is relatively safe. She can be taken to the veterinarian, operated on, and then be back in her whelping box at home within three hours, with all puppies nursing normally a short time later.

8. Health

WATCHING YOUR PUPPY'S HEALTH

First, don't be frightened by the number of diseases a dog can contract. The majority of dogs never get any of them. Don't become a dog-hypochondriac. All dogs have days when they feel lazy and want to lie around doing nothing. For the few diseases that you might be concerned about, remember that your veterinarian is your dog's best friend. When you first get your puppy, select a veterinarian who you feel is qualified to treat dogs. He will get to know your dog and will be glad to have you consult him for advice. A dog needs little medical care, but that little is essential to his good health and well-being. He needs:

1. Proper diet at regular hours
2. Clean, roomy housing
3. Daily exercise
4. Companionship and love
5. Frequent grooming
6. Regular check-ups by your veterinarian

THE USEFUL THERMOMETER

Almost every serious ailment shows itself by an increase in the dog's body temperature. If your dog acts lifeless, looks dull-eyed, and gives the impression of illness, check his temperature by using a rectal thermometer. Hold the dog and insert the thermometer, which should be lubricated with vaseline, and take a reading. The average normal temperature is 101.5° F. Excitement may raise this value slightly, but any rise of more than a few points is a cause for alarm. Consult your veterinarian.

FIRST AID

In general, a dog will heal his wounds by licking them. If he swallows anything harmful, chances are that he will throw it up. But it will probably make you feel better to help him if he is hurt, so treat his wounds as you would your own. Wash out the dirt and apply an antiseptic. If you are afraid that your dog has swallowed poison and you can't get to the veterinarian fast enough try to induce vomiting by giving him a strong solution of salt water or mustard and water. Amateur diagnosis is dangerous, because the symptoms of so many dog diseases are alike. Too many people wait too long to take their dog to the doctor.

IMPORTANCE OF INOCULATIONS

With the proper series of inoculations, your dog will be almost completely protected against disease. However, it occasionally happens that the shot does not take, and sometimes a different form of the virus appears against which your dog may not be protected.

DISTEMPER

Probably the most virulent of all dog diseases is distemper. Young dogs are most susceptible to it, although it may affect dogs of all ages. The dog will lose his appetite, seem depressed, chilled, and run a fever. Often he will have a watery discharge from his eyes and nose. Unless treated promptly, the disease goes into advanced stages with infections of the lungs, intestines, and nervous system, and dogs that recover may be left with some impairment such as paralysis, convulsions, a twitch, or some other defect, usually spastic in nature. The best protection against this is very early inoculation with a series of permanent shots and a booster shot each year thereafter.

HEPATITIS

Veterinarians report an increase in the spread of this viral disease in recent years, usually with younger dogs as the victims. The initial symptoms —drowsiness, vomiting, great thirst, loss of appetite, and a high temperature—closely resemble those of distemper. These symptoms are often accompanied by swellings of the head, neck, and abdomen. The disease strikes quickly; death may occur in just a few hours. Protection is afforded by injection with a vaccine recently developed.

LEPTOSPIROSIS

This disease is caused by bacteria that live in stagnant or slow-moving water. It is carried by rats and dogs; infection is begun by the dog's licking substances contaminated by the urine or feces of infected animals. The symptoms are diarrhea and a yellowish-brown discoloration of the jaws, tongue, and teeth, caused by an inflammation of the kidneys. This disease can be cured if caught in time, but it is best to ward it off with a vaccine which your veterinarian can administer along with the distemper shots.

RABIES

This is an acute disease of the dog's central nervous system. It is spread by infectious saliva transmitted by the bite of an infected animal. Rabies is generally manifested in one of two classes of symptoms. The first is "furious rabies," in which the dog shows a period of melancholy or depression, then irritation, and finally paralysis. The first period lasts from a few hours to several days. During this time the dog is cross and will change his position often. He loses his appetite for food and begins to lick, bite, and swallow foreign objects. During the irritative phase the dog is spasmodically wild and has impulses to run away. He acts in a fearless manner and runs and bites at everything in sight. If he is caged or confined he will fight at the bars, often breaking teeth or fracturing his jaw. His bark becomes a peculiar howl. In the final, or paralytic stage,, the animal's lower jaw becomes paralyzed and hangs down; he walks with a stagger and saliva drips from his mouth. Within four to eight days after the onset of paralysis, the dog dies.

The second class of symptoms is referred to as "dumb rabies" and is characterized by the dog's walking in a bearlike manner, head down. The lower jaw is paralyzed and the dog is unable to bite. Outwardly it may seem as though he had a bone caught in his throat.

Even if your pet should be bitten by a rabid dog or other animal, he probably can be saved if you get him to the veterinarian in time for a series of injections. However, after the symptoms have appeared no cure is possible. But remember that an annual rabies inoculation is almost certain protection against rabies. If you suspect your dog of having rabies, notify your local Health Department. A rabid dog is a danger to all who come near him.

As a rule, a puppy under four months of age cannot really be housetrained, but he can be broken to paper until he has enough control to be able to make exclusive use of the outdoors.

A proper performance by the puppy should bring forth lavish praise from the owner. Dogs learn by repetition; they will continue to perform those acts which have pleasant results and avoid doing the things that bring any sort of punishment.

When a puppy has learned to perform outdoors on a lead he may be truly considered as housebroken and trustworthy indoors.

COUGHS, COLDS, BRONCHITIS, PNEUMONIA

Respiratory diseases may affect the dog because he is forced to live under man-made conditions rather than in his natural environment. Being subjected to cold or a draft after a bath, sleeping near an air conditioner or in the path of a fan or near a radiator can cause respiratory ailments. The symptoms are similar to those in humans. The germs of these diseases, however, are different and do not affect both dogs and humans, so they cannot be infected by each other. Treatment is much the same as for a child with the same type of illness. Keep the dog warm, quiet, and well fed. Your veterinarian has antibiotics and other remedies to help the dog recover.

INTERNAL PARASITES

There are four common internal parasites that may infect your dog. These are roundworms, hookworms, whipworms, and tapeworms. The first three can be diagnosed by laboratory examination; the presence of tapeworms is determined by seeing segments in the stool or attached to the hair around the tail. Do not under any circumstances attempt to worm your dog without the advice of your veterinarian. After first determining what type of worm or worms are present, he will advise you of the best method of treatment.

EXTERNAL PARASITES

The dog that is groomed regularly and provided with clean sleeping quarters should not be troubled by fleas, ticks, or lice. If the dog should become infested with any of these parasites, he should be treated with a medicated dip bath or the new oral medications that are presently available.

SKIN AILMENTS

Any persistent scratching may indicate an irritation. Whenever you groom your dog, look for the reddish spots that may indicate eczema, mange, or fungal infection. Rather than treating your dog yourself, take him to the veterinarian, as some of the conditions may be difficult to eradicate.

EYES, EARS, TEETH, AND CLAWS

If you notice foreign matter collecting in the corners of your dog's eyes, wipe it out with a piece of cotton or tissue. If there is a discharge, check with your veterinarian.

Examine your dog's ears daily. Remove all visible wax, using a piece of cotton dipped in a boric acid solution or a solution of equal parts of water and hydrogen peroxide. Be gentle and don't probe into the ear, but just clean the parts you can see. If your dog continually shakes his head and twitches or scratches his ears, it is best to have the veterinarian take a look.

If you give your dog a hard chewing toy made of rawhide or nylon— the kind you can buy at the pet shop—it will serve him the same way a toothbrush serves you and will prevent the accumulation of tartar on his teeth. Check his mouth regularly, and take him to the veterinarian if you find collected tartar or bloody spots on his gums. As your dog gets older he should have his teeth cleaned once a year. Do not give your dog bones; he can choke or puncture his bowels on them.

To clip your dog's claws, use specially designed clippers that are available at your pet shop. Never take off too much of the claw, as you might cut the quick, which is sensitive and will bleed. Be particularly careful when you cut claws in which the quick is not visible. If you have any doubts about being able to cut your dog's claws, have your veterinarian or pet shop do it periodically.

CARE OF THE AGED DOG

With the increased knowledge and care available, there is no reason why your dog should not live to a good old age. As the years go by he may need a little additional care. Remember that an excessively fat dog is not healthy, particularly as he grows older, so limit the older dog's food accordingly. He needs exercise as much as ever, although his heart cannot bear the strain of sudden and violent exertion. Failing eyesight or hearing means lessened awareness of dangers, so you must protect him more than ever.

Should you decide at this time to get a puppy, to avoid being without a dog when your old friend is no longer with you, be very careful how you introduce the puppy. He naturally will be playful and will expect the older dog to respond to his advances. Sometimes the old dog will get a new lease on life from a new puppy, but he may be consumed with jealousy. Do not give the newcomer the attention that formerly was exclusively the older dog's. Feed them apart, and show your old friend that you still love him the most; the puppy, not being accustomed to individual attention, will not mind sharing your love.

BIBLIOGRAPHY

Breed Your Dog, Dr. Leon Whitney, 64 pp.,   Illustrated throughout with instructive photographs in both color and black and white. Covers aspects of breeding through puppyhood.

Dollars in Dogs, Leon F. Whitney, D.V.M., 255 pp.,   Twenty-six chapters on different vocations in the vast field of dog business. An excellent book for your library.

First Aid For Your Dog, Dr. Herbert Richards, 64 pp.,   Illustrated throughout in both color and black and white.

Groom Your Dog, Leon F. Whitney, D.V.M., 64 pp.,   Illustrated throughout with both color and black and white photographs showing various grooming techniques.

How to Feed Your Dog, Dr. Leon F. Whitney, 64 pp.,   Best diets and feeding routines for puppies and adult canines. Profusely illustrated in color and black and white.

How To Housebreak And Train Your Dog, Arthur Liebers, 80 pp., Six educational chapters on training your dog. Illustrated in color and black and white photographs.

How To Raise And Train A Pedigreed Or Mixed Breed Puppy, Arthur Liebers, 64 pp.,   Nine chapters covering such canine questions as choosing your puppy through breeding the adult. Illustrated in both color and black and white photographs.

The Distemper Complex, Leon F. Whitney, D.V.M., and George D. Whitney, D.V.M., 219 pp.,   A comprehensive canine health book. Nineteen revealing chapters. A thirty-nine-page bibliography. Completely indexed.

This Is The Puppy, Ernest Hart, 190 pp.,   Eleven profusely-illustrated chapters to guide the reader in the care and selection of a puppy. Full-color photographs. Also black and white candids. Indexed.